Let's grow

Written by Barbara Taylor
Photography by Steve Teague

Bath · New York · Singapore · Hong Kong · Cologne · Delhi
Melbourne · Amsterdam · Johannesburg · Auckland · Shenzhen

With special thanks to our models Jake Beltran, Harry Goddard, Ruby Goddard, Ellie Morgan, Chloe Meek and Meg Teague.

Plant and garden growers: Naomi and Steve Teague

Pumpkin photo credit: 14bl © Dave Reede/Corbis

This edition published by Parragon in 2011

Parragon
Queen Street House
4 Queen Street
Bath BA1 1HE, UK
www.parragon.com

ISBN 978-1-4454-6438-1

Printed in China

Contents

The Magic of Plants

Everyone loves looking at beautiful flowers or eating delicious vegetables, but growing them can be even more fun. Growing plants is a kind of magic. A small sunflower seed can grow taller than you, a papery brown bulb sprouts into a beautiful hyacinth and a green shoot snipped off a Forsythia bush grows into a completely new plant!

To be good at growing plants, you need to understand what they need to survive (see pages 6 and 7) and follow the growing steps carefully. Ask an adult to help you buy the plants and growing materials. Take a few minutes to read these pages and then you'll be ready to **start growing**!

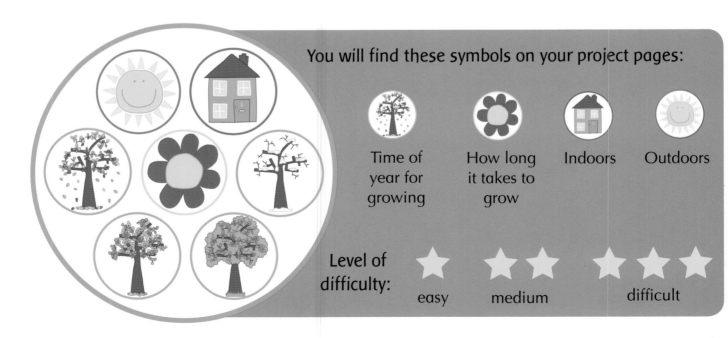

You will find these symbols on your project pages:

Time of year for growing

How long it takes to grow

Indoors

Outdoors

Level of difficulty:

easy   medium   difficult

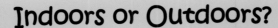

Indoors or Outdoors?

If you have your own patch of garden in which to grow your plants, that's great! But you don't need a garden for many of the growing projects in this book. A lot of the plants can be grown indoors on a windowsill or outdoors on a balcony, patio or any small paved area. If you only have a small area, choose small plants. (Read the seed packets or the labels in garden centres carefully.)

Safety First!

• Look out for the ⚠ symbol in the projects. When you see this, ask for adult help to:

– use a sharp knife or scissors
– dig and clear the soil in the garden
– move heavy growbags
– make holes in containers for drainage
– bend sharp garden wire
– pick up prickly plants, such as cacti
– identify poisonous plants

• Always wear gloves when handling thorny or prickly plants or plants with sharp leaves.
• Never walk around with a sharp knife or scissors in your hands.
• Use a kneeling mat if kneeling for a long time.
• Always wash any food plants you have grown before eating them.
• Clear away any dog or cat mess.

Clean and Tidy

• Wash your hands after touching plants and soil.
• Wear old clothes or overalls in case you get muddy.
• Wear sunscreen when outdoors for a long time.

Growing Tips

Here are a few useful tips about some of the basic skills you will need to grow and look after the plants in this book. Different kinds of plants need different growing conditions. Make sure you read the seed packets or plant labels carefully. They will tell you how much light and water each plant needs, and what sort of soil will be most suitable for healthy growth. They will also tell you when to plant seeds, how big a plant will grow and when it will flower.

Light and Shade

Plants need light to make the food they use to live and grow.
If you leave plants in the dark, they will die.

 Some plants, such as sunflowers, like to grow in full sunlight.

 Other plants, such as ferns, prefer to grow in the shade.

Watering

Plants drink water through their roots. They use the water to help them make their food and stay alive.

• When you first put a plant or a seed in soil or compost, water it well to encourage the roots to grow.
• A watering can with a spray on the spout is good for spreading water over a wide area.
• Be careful not to over-water your plants. Remember, rainwater is better for plants than tap water!
• Check your plants about once a week to make sure they have enough water. With most plants the soil should be damp to the touch.
• Add gravel or pebbles to the bottom of a plant pot and make sure there are drainage holes in the bottom. This prevents the roots getting waterlogged.

Bottle Spray

For watering seeds and very small plants, it's best to use a fine mist spray from a bottle. That way you won't wash away the seeds or damage delicate plants.

Compost

The compost you buy from garden centres contains a good mix of nutrients (food substances) for growing plants, with no pests or diseases in it.

- Choose the right sort of compost. There is one for seeds, one for cuttings and another one for bigger plants with roots.
- You can make your own compost from vegetable scraps, paper, leaves and grass clippings.

Support

- Tall plants with thin stems may need to be tied to canes to stop them falling over.
- Climbing plants may be able to climb up a fence or a trellis, or wind themselves around other plants.

Trimming...

- It's a good idea to cut off dead leaves because they may become mouldy and spread diseases.
- You may want to trim your plants to control their shape. If you want the shoot to keep growing, make a neat cut just above a bud.

and Tidying

- Cutting off seed heads will encourage plants to grow new leaves instead of using up energy making their seeds.
- You may want to leave some seed heads to develop so you can collect the seeds and plant them the next year.

Tallest Sunflowers

Spring/Summer

4–5 months

Wow!
Would you like to
grow a flower that's
taller than you?
Sunflowers may start
off as tiny seeds but they
end up as giant flowers!
Who can grow the
tallest one?

What you need:

- 3 sunflower seeds
- Gloves
- Soil
- Fork
- 3 × 2-litre plastic
  bottles, cut in half
- Bamboo canes
- Garden string

1  Find a sunny, sheltered patch of soil. Clear away the stones and weeds.

2  Using a fork, make 3 holes, 2 cm deep. Drop a seed into each hole and cover it with soil.

3  Put the plastic bottles over the seeds.

4  Water the seeds daily. Seedlings will show in about 21 days. Once they look strong, remove the bottles.

DID YOU KNOW?

When the seeds form in the middle of your sunflower, watch out for birds coming to eat them. Collect some seeds and store them in a dry envelope, ready to plant for next year!

TIP: To grow very tall sunflowers, choose the ones with the strongest stems and the biggest, greenest leaves.

5 When the sunflowers begin to get tall, push a bamboo cane next to each plant and tie the stem loosely to the cane.

6 After about 12 weeks, the sunflowers will start to flower. Keep watering them and watch them grow!

9

Sweet Pea Tepee

Spring/Summer

4–5 months

A frame full of flowers is a great way to brighten up your patio! It doesn't take up much space, and you can even cut bunches of flowers to decorate your home or give to your friends or family.

What you need:
- 6 sweet pea seeds
- Jar
- Large pot
- Compost
- 3 bamboo canes
- Garden string
- Dibber
- Gloves

10

1
Soak the seeds overnight in water to soften the hard seed coat before planting.

2
Put a large pot in a sunny, sheltered spot. Fill it almost to the top with compost.

3
Push 3 bamboo canes into the pot. Tie them together at the top to make a tepee frame.

4
Use a dibber to make a small hole at the base of each cane. Put 2 seeds into each hole. Cover with compost.

5
Keep the compost moist. When the shoots appear, gently wind them around the frame. Keep winding the plants around each cane as they climb.

6
After 12–16 weeks the sweet peas will flower, with a lovely scent.

DID YOU KNOW?

Sweet peas have thin curly tendrils, which wind around things and stop the plants falling down. Clever, huh?

Tasty Tomatoes

Spring/Autumn

5–6 months

There's nothing quite as satisfying as eating tomatoes that you've grown yourself. Tomatoes love to grow in sunny spots and need plenty of water! The perfect thing to grow outdoors!

What you need:

- 3 tomato plants
- Gloves
- Trowel
- Bamboo canes
- Garden string
- Paintbrush
- Tomato fertilizer

1

Put the growbag by a sunny wall. Make 3 slits 15 cm apart. Put a tomato plant in each slit. Pat compost round the roots. ⚠

2

Check the compost daily to see if it needs watering. Once a week, add 2 drops of tomato fertilizer to your watering can and water.

3

When the plants are 30 cm tall, push a bamboo cane next to each plant. Tie the plant stem loosely to the cane.

4

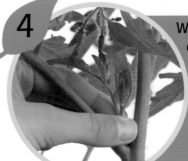

With your thumb and finger, pinch out any side shoots that grow between the leaves and the main stem.

TIP: For extra satisfaction, try growing your tomatoes from seed next time, rather than buying the young plants.

5 When the flowers open, gently tickle the centre of each flower with a paintbrush to help them pollinate.

6 When the plants have flowered, the base of the flowers swell into baby green tomatoes. Wait for them to ripen.

13

Perfect Pumpkins

Spring/Autumn

7–8 months

Why not grow a spooky pumpkin for your Halloween lantern? Pumpkins can grow almost anywhere, all they need is room to grow. Although they aren't the quickest, they are well worth the wait!

What you need:

- 2 pumpkin seedlings
- Soil
- Trowel
- Gloves
- Straw
- Liquid feed

14

1  Find a sunny, sheltered patch of soil. Clear away the stones and weeds.

2  Make 2 small mounds about 5 cm high. Place a pumpkin seedling into each mound and press the soil down firmly.

3  Water the plant every other day. Add some liquid feed (read the label first) to your watering can once a week.

4  After 6 weeks, the plant will flower. Pinch out flowers, leaving 2 or 3. When there are 5 big leaves, pinch out the shoot ends.

5  When the plant has flowered, the fruit will form. Put some straw on the ground under the fruit to stop it from spoiling.

6  When you are happy with the size of your pumpkin, trim it off. Put it in a light place for about 10 days until the skin hardens.

TIP: In the autumn, when your pumpkin is ready to pick, ask an adult to help you scoop out the insides. Save the seeds for sowing next year, and use the flesh to make soups and yummy pies.

Ivy Letters

Who needs a pen to write with when you can make letters out of plants? Ivy is a good plant to use for this because it has little roots along its stems, which cling tightly to things. It's as easy as ABC!

What you need:

- Ivy cuttings
- Pot with drainage hole
- Compost
- Gloves
- Trowel
- Garden wire
- Tape
- Scissors

1  Put a large pot in a sunny, sheltered spot. Fill to within 2 cm of the top with compost.

2 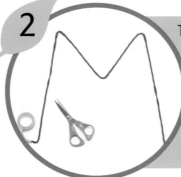 Twist together 2–3 strands of garden wire, then bend into a letter. Leave 2 'feet' at the bottom. Tape the sharp ends.

3  Push the wire letter into the pot. Press the compost firmly around the letter 'feet'.

4  Take 2 ivy cuttings about 7 cm long. Push a cut stem into the pot at each end of the wire.

TIP: If you trim the ivy, it will grow more thickly. If you want a quick fix, buy some ivy with a long trail and get instant satisfaction!

5 Gently wind the stems around the wire frame to help the plants climb around it.

6 Check the compost daily to see if it needs watering. Trim any side shoots carefully with scissors so you can see the shape of the letter. ⚠

17

Strawberry Boots

Spring/Summer

2–3 months

Strawberries are one of the juiciest fruits to grow. They love the summer sunshine and by growing them in a boot you will keep away unwanted slugs. Your own freshly picked strawberries will disappear faster than you can say: "I grew these!"

What you need:

- Strawberry plants
- Old rubber boot
- Scissors
- Gloves
- Compost
- Netting
- Straw

18

1  Ask an adult to cut some small holes in the side of an old rubber boot. Make a few holes in the sole for drainage. ⚠️

2 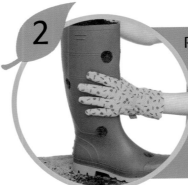 Put the boot outside in a sunny, sheltered spot. Fill the boot with compost.

3  Put 1 strawberry plant in each hole and 2 or 3 plants at the top of the boot.

4  Water the strawberries but make sure you don't over-water them.

5  Protect the plants from birds and slugs with netting. The fruits will start off green or white before they ripen.

6  When the fruit start to trail, put some straw underneath to stop them from spoiling.

TIP: Strawberry plants will produce fruit for 3–4 summers, but then you will need to replace them.

19

Cress Caterpillar

Have you ever seen one of those hairy, scary caterpillars? Have fun making a big green caterpillar with 'hair' made out of cress shoots. You can even eat the cress when the caterpillar's 'hair' grows long enough!

What you need:

- Cotton wool roll
- Egg carton
- Mustard and cress seeds
- Black marker pen
- Scissors

20

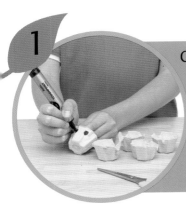

1 Cut the egg carton into 6 separate cups. Draw a face on one of the cups with the marker pen. ⚠️

2 Dampen some cotton wool. Put a small piece of the cotton wool in the bottom of each empty egg cup.

3 Sprinkle the cotton wool with mustard seeds and cress seeds.

4 Put the caterpillar egg cups in a light, warm place. Make sure you keep the cotton wool damp.

5 Check on the seeds every day. After a couple of days, you will see little shoots begin to sprout.

6 After about 10 days, the cress will be long. Cut the cress hair, then wash it and put it in your sandwiches or salad! ⚠️

TIP: When you have eaten all the cress, plant some more seeds to make an everlasting sandwich filler.

21

Crazy Hair Day

All seasons

2–3 weeks

You'll have a wicked time giving grass a crazy haircut! Get creative with your scissors – how many different styles can you think of? Use hair ties or slides to hold your grass 'hair' in place.

What you need:

- 4 different-sized plastic flower pots
- Funny face stickers
- Glass jar
- Trowel
- Gravel
- Seed compost
- Different types of grass seed, such as lawn seed, feather grass, Blue Fescue and Evergold
- Scissors

1

Put the seeds in a clean glass jar and add some water. Soak the seeds overnight in a cool place.

2

Put some gravel in the bottom of each pot to help with drainage. Decorate each pot with the stickers.

3

Almost fill each pot with compost.

4

Sprinkle a handful of seeds on the surface of each pot. Put a different type of seed in each pot.

22

Here are some style ideas:
- Short and spiky
- Crazy coifs
- Mohican look
- Braids or knots
- Trailing layers
- Pretty ponytails

5 Leave the pots in a light place and keep the compost moist.

6  After about 10 days, start trimming the grassy hair. Give each pot a different funky haircut!

23

Windowsill Salad

When you're in a hurry, a salad is a great way to make a quick meal that's really good for you! It's even better if you've grown the green stuff yourself.

What you need:
- Window box
- Gravel
- Seed compost
- Trowel
- Seeds for salad, such as lettuce, radish, spring onions
- Plant labels
- Marker pen

1 Put some gravel in the bottom of the window box. Fill it about three-quarters full with the seed compost.

2 Scatter the seeds thinly on the surface of the compost. Put each kind of seed in a different area of the box.

3 Cover the seeds with a thin layer of the compost and label each area with the name of the seed.

4 Leave the window box in a light place and water the compost regularly.

5 When the seeds start to sprout, pull out the spindly ones so the stronger plants have more room to grow.

6 After a few weeks, your salad should be ready to eat!

TIP: You can make your own plant labels from ice-lolly sticks, or cut strips from empty yoghurt pots.

Balancing Bulbs

Winter/Spring

Up to 15 weeks

With its dry, wrinkly skin, a hyacinth bulb may look boring, but a wonderful surprise is hidden inside. If you look after it well, it will sprout a beautiful spike of scented flowers. Hyacinth flowers come in a variety of colours – and they make a great gift!

What you need:
- Hyacinth bulb
- Jug
- Clean jam jar
- Gloves
- Toothpicks

1

Almost fill an empty jam jar to the top with some cold water.

2

Push four toothpicks into the side of the fattest part of the hyacinth bulb.

3

Balance the bulb on top of the jar with the fat end of the bulb just above the water.

4

Put the jar in a cool, dark place and keep it topped up with water.

TIP: When the flowers turn brown, cut off the flowering spike. Leave the green leaves so they can make food that will be stored in the bulb for next year. When the leaves die, cut them off too. Store the bulb in a cool, dry place until next spring – then it will flower all over again!

TIP: Wear gloves when touching the bulb because it might irritate your skin and cause a rash.

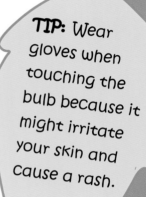

5

When a shoot pushes out of the top of the bulb and the roots are about 10 cm long, move the jar into a warm, light place.

6

Watch the bud open and flower. It will give off a lovely scent.

27

Floating Forest

Let your imagination go wild! This floating forest is a great place to escape into a mini-world of adventure and discovery. Will it be monsters or mermaids? Only you can decide...

What you need:
- Big plastic plate or tray
- Tops of vegetables and fruits, such as carrots, parsnips, turnips and pineapples
- Water
- Toy animals

1 Cut the tops off some vegetables or use the trimmings left over when an adult is preparing vegetables for a meal. ⚠

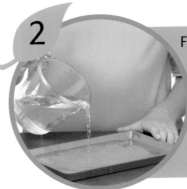

2 Fill the plastic plate or tray with a shallow layer of water.

3 Float your veggie tops on the water with the cut edge down.

4 Leave the plate or tray in a light, warm place and wait for the shoots and leaves to sprout.

5 Keep the water topped up.

6 Once the leaves are tall enough, you will have a floating forest where you can play with your toy animals.

TIP: Don't keep your floating forest too long, or the veggie tops will start to go mouldy.

Herb Fun

All seasons

1–3 weeks

Herbs smell and taste delicious. There are lots to choose from. Try growing thyme, rosemary, dill and mint to flavour your food, or make scented herb bags as a special gift.

What you need:

- Herb plants, such as mint, oregano, thyme, sage, marjoram and rosemary
- Metal or plastic container
- Compost
- Plant labels
- Trowel
- Gloves
- Gravel
- Pebbles

1  Put some pebbles in the bottom of the container and fill it half way up with compost.

2  Make a label for each different herb to help you remember their names.

3  Tap the pots to loosen the plants, then lift them out. Put one herb plant in each corner of the container.

4  Leave the mint plant in its pot and place in the middle of the container. Fill in the gaps with compost and press down firmly.

Golden Thyme

Golden

Mint

Oregano

Sage

5

Sprinkle the gravel on top of the compost to make a pattern. Put a plant label next to each herb.

TIP: Herb leaves can be either picked and used straight away or dried so they will keep for a long time. To dry herbs, tie them in bunches and hang them upside down in an airy, warm place for a few weeks. Store dried herbs in a clean jar with a lid.

6

Place your herb garden in a warm, sheltered spot. Remember to water the compost regularly.

Fairy Flowers

Spring/Summer

2–5 weeks

Make a pretty garden for tiny fairies! Choose some annual plants that have small flowers, such as alyssum, lobelia, morning glory, nasturtium, pansy, primula and zinnia.

What you need:
- Annual flowering plants
- Garden trug
- Plastic bag
- Small pebbles
- Toy fairies
- Compost
- Trowel
- Windmill
- Jar lid
- Dibber

1 Line the bottom of the trug with a plastic bag so that the water won't drain through. ⚠

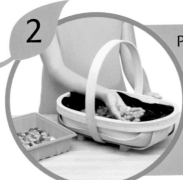

2 Put pebbles in the bottom and half fill with compost. Put the jar lid upside down in the trug to look like a pond.

3 Use a dibber to make some holes in the compost, leaving spaces in-between for the plants. ⚠

4 Tap the pots then lift out the plants. Place in the holes. Sprinkle compost around the plants and press down firmly.

5 Hide your toy fairies among the flowers. Then add a colourful windmill.

6 Carry your flower garden to a sunny spot. Don't forget to water your flower garden regularly.

TIP: If you have a favourite colour, why not choose flowers that are all one colour? How many different plants of one colour can you find?

33

Cactus Bucket

All seasons

1–3 weeks

Master the art of growing spiky cactus plants to bring the desert into your home. Once you start collecting, you'll be amazed at how many different kinds of cacti there are! The furry ones are really cool!

What you need:
- Tin bucket
- Cactus plants
- Bowl
- Pebbles
- Compost
- Sand
- Trowel
- Newspaper
- Gloves
- Gravel

1

Put some pebbles in the bottom of the bucket.

2

Mix some compost with the same amount of sand. Fill the bucket almost to the top with the mixture.

3

Wrap some folded newspaper around a cactus plant and tap the side of the pot gently to loosen it. Stand it in the bucket.

4

Pot all the plants, then sprinkle some more sand and compost mixture on top and pat it down firmly.

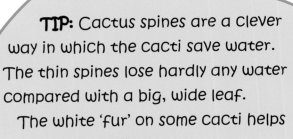

TIP: Cactus spines are a clever way in which the cacti save water. The thin spines lose hardly any water compared with a big, wide leaf. The white 'fur' on some cacti helps to protect them from cold desert nights.

5 Cover the surface with sand and gravel. Decorate your garden with pebbles.

6 Water the gravel at first, but after this, only water when the soil is dry. Remember, these plants come from deserts!

35

Rocky Garden

Spring/Summer

1–3 weeks

Choose three alpine plants with different flowers and leaves, such as saxifrages or houseleeks (*Sempervivum*); thrift or campion; pinks (*Dianthus*) or gentians.

What you need:

- Alpine plants
- Plastic container
- Pebbles or stones
- Sand
- Trowel
- Gravel

36

1
Put some pebbles in the bottom of the container and half fill it with sand.

2
Leave the plants in their pots and put them on top of the sand, leaving spaces in-between.

3
Now add some more sand so it comes half way up the pots.

4
Add a thick layer of gravel over the sand and the pots. Arrange some pebbles on top of the gravel.

5
Water the gravel around the plants to keep them moist, but not too wet.

6
Leave your alpine garden in a warm place, out of direct sunlight.

Sensory Surprise

Spring/Summer

1–4 weeks

You can smell, touch, taste and even listen to your garden! Choose one plant for each of these four senses. Try lavender for a delicious smell, lamb's ear for its fluffy leaves, chives for their oniony taste and *Nigella* for the sound of its seed heads.

What you need:

- Plants for each sense
- Deep plastic tray
- Compost
- Pebbles
- Trowel
- Dibber
- Gloves
- Blindfold

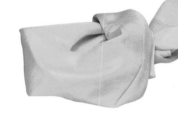

1 Put some pebbles in the bottom of the tray and half fill the tray with compost.

2 Use the dibber to make holes for the plants, leaving space between them.

3 Tap the plant pots gently to loosen the plants, then lift them into the holes.

4 Fill in the gaps with some more compost and pat it down firmly.

5 Leave your garden tray on a sunny windowsill. Remember to water it regularly.

6 Blindfold a friend and ask them to experience the scent, sound, taste and feel of your sensory garden!

Worms at Work

All seasons

2–4 weeks

Earthworms are good for gardens because they mix up the soil and their burrows let air and water into the soil. By eating dead leaves, worms help the leaves to rot and make the soil healthy. This helps plants to grow.

What you need:

- Large glass jar or plastic bottle
- Dead leaves
- Soil
- Sand
- 3–5 worms
- Gloves
- Trowel
- Dark cloth or black paper

1 Fill the glass jar with alternate layers of soil and sand, finishing with a layer of soil on top.

2 Lay some dead leaves on top of the soil and spray with water to make the soil moist. Worms die if they dry out.

3 Ask an adult to help you collect 3 to 5 worms from the garden. Be careful not to leave them out of the soil too long. ⚠

4 Put the worms on top of the soil. Watch them burrow down away from the light.

5 Cover the jar with a dark cloth or black paper. Leave your wormery in a dark place for a week.

6 Take off the covering to see how the worms have dragged the leaves into the soil to eat. The layers of soil and sand will look mixed up.

TIP: Don't forget to put the worms back into the garden afterwards!

Decorating Pots

Terracotta Pot

- Terracotta pot
- Saucer
- Shells
- Craft glue
- String
- 2 books

Step 1 – Put some craft glue into a saucer. Lay the pot on its side with a book each side to stop it rolling.

Step 2 – Dip each shell into the glue and place carefully in position on the pot. Wait for the glue to dry. Once dry, move the pot round and carry on sticking shells.

Step 3 – When all the shells are stuck on and the glue has dried, paint craft glue around the rim. Then stick the string round the top of the pot to finish it off.

Decorated Basket

- Basket with handle
- Ribbons
- Tissue paper
- Scissors
- Sticky tape

Step 1 – Decorate the handle with ribbon and tie bows through the weave on the sides.

Step 2 – For the flowers, make circles out of tissue paper. Then twist 5 cm squares of tissue into sticks for the stems. Fold the tissue circles in half and in half again. Cut the point off to make a small hole at the centre.

Step 3 – Thread onto a circle the twisted end and push along the stem, leaving a bit sticking out for the centre. Pinch the tissue around the stem and tape to hold in place. Do this twice more, then wind an extra bit of tape around the stem to make it firm.

Painted Yoghurt Pot

- Large yoghurt pot
- Acrylic paints
- Paintbrushes

Step 1 – Paint the whole pot white to cover any printing, then leave to dry.

Step 2 – Once dry, draw the main parts of your design onto the pot with a pencil. Paint your design in one colour at a time, leaving the paint to dry between colours. If you want to paint a light colour over a dark colour, paint a white layer first.

Painted Vase

- Clear plastic bottle
- Glass paints
- Paintbrush
- Scissors
- 2 books

Step 1 – Ask an adult to cut the top off the bottle. The line can be wavy or straight.

Step 2 – Lay the bottle on its side with a book each side to stop it rolling. Paint flowers on one side of the bottle and leave to dry. Keep rolling the bottle round and painting until you've covered all the way round. Let the paint dry before you use the vase.

Sticker Pot

- Plastic pot
- Stickers
- PVA glue
- Paintbrush

Step 1 – Decorate the pot with stickers, sticking them anywhere you like.

Step 2 – To make the pot waterproof, paint the pot with PVA glue. Leave to dry before using.

Taking Cuttings

1

To make new plants, ask an adult to help you cut off the tips of side shoots or young stems without any flowers. Make each cut just below a leaf. ⚠

What you need:
- Plants, such as begonias, Michaelmas daisies, geraniums or rosemary
- Flowerpots or yoghurt pots
- Compost
- Scissors
- Rooting powder
- Plastic bags
- Elastic bands or string

2

Carefully pull off the lower leaves and stand the cuttings in water until they grow roots. To encourage rooting, dip the cut ends in rooting powder.

3

Fill some pots with compost and plant 3 or 4 cuttings in a pot. Press down the compost firmly around each cutting.

4

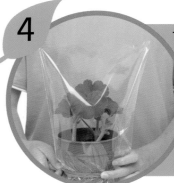

To keep the cuttings warm and moist, cover the pots with plastic bags. Hold the bag in place with an elastic band or string.

potting On

TIP: If you grow plants indoors, they will bend towards the light to get as much light as possible. Outside, some plants (such as sunflowers) even turn to follow the Sun as it moves across the sky.

1

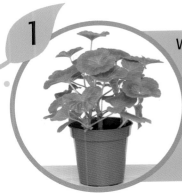

Wait for the cuttings to grow new leaves. This means that the plants are strong and healthy and are growing roots.

2

Move each cutting to a small pot of its own. Try not to damage the roots as you pull the cuttings carefully out of their old pots.

3

Fill the new pots with compost. Make a hole in the middle and pot the cuttings. Add compost and press down firmly around each cutting.

4

Water the cuttings and keep them warm and moist. When they are strong enough, plant them outside in the garden.

Garden Tools

Fork

Flowerpots

Watering can

Dibber

Plant labels

Spray bottle

Trowel

Spade

Seed trays

Bucket

Gloves

Gardening Words

Alpines
Small mountain plants, which grow higher up the mountain than trees.

Bud
A small bump on a plant's stem from which a shoot, a leaf or a flower develops.

Bulb
A rounded, underground stem wrapped in layers of leaves that contains stored food.

Compost
A substance made from rotted materials, which helps to make the soil healthy.

Cutting
A piece of a growing plant, such as a shoot, which is cut off to start a new plant.

Deadheading
Carefully pulling the dead flowers from plants to encourage new flowers to grow.

Nutrients
Chemical substances in the soil, which plants need to live and grow.

Root
The underground part of a plant that takes up water and nutrients.

Runner
A long, creeping stem, which sprouts baby plants along its length.

Secateurs
Sharp gardening clippers, which are used for trimming plants.

Seed
A structure made by flowers, which contains a baby plant and a food store wrapped in a protective coat.

Shoot
A new growth that sprouts from a plant, or the first growth from a seed above the soil.

Sprout
To start growing, such as a shoot sprouting from a seed.

Stem
The part of a plant that holds the leaves above the soil. Tubes inside the stem carry water and plant foods.

Tendril
A special winding stem, which climbing plants use to support themselves.

Index